NEVER SILENT

A HIROSHIMA SURVIVOR'S STORY

Written by **Setsuko Thurlow and Kathy Lowinger**

Illustrated by **Michelle Theodore**

annick press
toronto • berkeley

© 2025 Setsuko Thurlow and Kathy Lowinger (text)
© 2025 Michelle Theodore (illustrations)

Cover art by Michelle Theodore, designed by Danielle Arbour
Interior designed by Danielle Arbour

Edited by Linda Pruessen
Copyedited by Eleanor Gasparik
Proofread by Catherine Dorton

Annick Press and its logo are registered trademarks of Annick Press Ltd.

Annick Press supports the copyright of the creators of this work. As readers buying authorized editions of this book and complying with copyright law you do likewise. All rights are reserved without the permission of the copyright holder and publisher. These uses include reproducing, storing, training, retrieving, and transmitting in any form including electronic, mechanical, photocopying, recording, or otherwise. Distributing this work online is illegal and punishable by law. Your support of the creators of this work is appreciated.

This book is funded in part by the Government of Canada. *Ce livre est financé en partie par le gouvernement du Canada.* We acknowledge the support of the Canada Council for the Arts. *Nous remercions le Conseil des arts du Canada de son soutien.* We would like to acknowledge the funding support of the Ontario Arts Council (OAC) and the Government of Ontario for their support. We also acknowledge the support of the Government of Ontario through the Ontario Book Publishing Tax Credit, and through Ontario Creates.

Library and Archives Canada Cataloguing in Publication

Title: Never silent : a Hiroshima survivor's story / written by Setsuko Thurlow and Kathy Lowinger ; illustrated by Michelle Theodore.
Names: Thurlow, Setsuko, author | Lowinger, Kathy, author | Theodore, Michelle, illustrator
Identifiers: Canadiana (print) 20250128713 | Canadiana (ebook) 20250128950 | ISBN 9781773219851 (hardcover) | ISBN 9781773219875 (EPUB) | ISBN 9781773219882 (PDF)
Subjects: LCSH: Thurlow, Setsuko—Juvenile literature. | LCSH: Thurlow, Setsuko—Childhood and youth—Juvenile literature. | LCSH: Thurlow, Setsuko—Political activity—Canada—Juvenile literature. | LCSH: Atomic bomb victims—Japan—Hiroshima-shi—Biography—Juvenile literature. | LCSH: Hiroshima-shi (Japan)—History—Bombardment, 1945—Juvenile literature. | CSH: Japanese Canadians—Biography—Juvenile literature. | LCSH: Japanese—Canada—Biography—Juvenile literature. | LCSH: Nuclear disarmament—Juvenile literature. LCGFT: Autobiographies. | LCGFT: Biographies.
Classification: LCC D767.25.H6 T58 2025 | DDC j940.54/2521954092—dc23

Published in the U.S.A. by Annick Press (U.S.) Ltd.
Distributed in Canada by University of Toronto Press.
Distributed in the U.S.A. by Publishers Group West.

Printed in Canada

annickpress.com | michelletheodore.com

Contents

A Message from Setsuko   7

The Before Time   9
Daughter of a Samurai   10
Everything Changes   12
War Comes to Japan   15
A Visit to Hiroshima   16
The World Goes to War, 1939–1945   20
Japan in World War II   22
Hardships of Daily Life   24

"The Most Terrible Bomb"   27
A Silent Flash   28
The Living and the Dead   30
The Days After   34
Surrender   37
Numb   38
Life Under Occupation   40
A New Kind of Weapon   43
Little Boy and Fat Man   44

"The Silence Lifts"   49
The Hibakusha   50
The Atomic Age Is Born   52
A New Focus   54
My Fight for Peace   57
Ban the Bomb!   60
A Call to Action   61

Appendix: Japan at War Timeline   62
Sources   64
Credits   64

"Don't give up! Crawl toward the light!"

The man's voice was urgent. He grabbed my shoulder as I struggled through the rubble that covered me. The wooden building where thirty of us had been working was in flames.

A Message from Setsuko

At 8:15 on the morning of August 6, 1945, the United States dropped an atomic bomb on the city of Hiroshima. It unleashed horrific destruction. Most of the men had gone off to war. That awful day, seventy thousand women, children, and old people were incinerated, carbonized, and vaporized. By the end of 1945, another seventy thousand had perished. Among them were members of my own family and 351 of my schoolmates. Each had a life, a future, people who loved them—all erased in an instant. The horror of that day, and of the days, months, and years of suffering that followed, is almost impossible to describe. Over the years, many thousands more would die, often in mysterious ways that we would come to learn were the effects of radiation. To this day, radiation is still killing survivors. We don't know what the genetic effect will be on our children and grandchildren.

I am telling you this story not because I want your pity. I am writing to encourage you to act.

—From notes for Setsuko Thurlow's speech in Oslo in 2017, when the International Campaign to Abolish Nuclear Weapons was awarded the Nobel Peace Prize

The Before Time

Daughter of a Samurai

I was born Setsuko Nakamura in Kojijn-machi, an eastern part of Hiroshima, on January 3, 1932, into a samurai family.

Though the privileges that had once come with being a samurai were gone by this time, there was still honor. Our house had a marker outside so that people would know that a samurai family lived there.

I was proud of being from a samurai family, and my mother made sure I knew that with the privilege came responsibility to society. She was a devout Buddhist. Buddhists believe that though there is suffering in human life, enlightenment can be achieved through spiritual and physical labor and good behavior. I grew up watching my mother carry out many acts of worship and charity.

Setsuko at thirteen

Two samurai pose with their swords in 1877.

The Samurai

The samurai were an elite class of fearless warriors in Japan from the twelfth to the nineteenth century. Although emperors were the official rulers, the real power lay with the samurai. As well as being superb fighters, they were often artists. By the time Setsuko was born, samurai warriors no longer existed. The emperor Meiji had abolished the samurai system to change Japan into a more modern industrialized nation-state. In 1871, the samurai class was officially dissolved and samurai land was confiscated. Wearing a sword had been a visible privilege given only to samurai. Now it was forbidden.

Everything Changes

My six brothers and sisters were much older than I was. The gardener who tended our lovely garden became my friend, teaching me about the trees and flowers. My father was the head of the family—the clan—so relatives were always coming and going. They all doted on me, the precocious baby of the family.

Reading was my favorite thing. I read the newspapers and followed current events—there was always someone willing to answer my stream of questions.

School was easy for me. I was the only girl to get honors for each of the first six years of elementary school. From junior high on, I went to a private Christian girls' school, Hiroshima Jogakuin, noted for teaching English and music. If you kept up your marks, you could learn to play the piano. I longed for that.

The war changed everything.

Setsuko, second from left, at age fourteen, with her parents (mother to her right, father to her left), sister (standing behind her), sister-in-law, and niece (to her father's left)

War Comes to Japan

I can say that my childhood ended on December 8, 1941. That day, the radio announcer declared that Japan was at war with the United States and the Allied forces.

The radio announcers reminded us of our commitment to the emperor. Every day, year after year, we listened to the radio for news about the war. First would come stirring music. Then we would get reports of the battles we had won.

I was in eighth grade. Along with about thirty girls from my school, I was given special training to help decode messages from the front lines. It was complicated work. You had to add and subtract quickly and check the code books fast without making any mistakes. It shows how desperate Japan was that schoolgirls were put in charge of such important work. What we didn't know was that the Americans had broken the codes.

As summer wore on, everyone was tense. Other cities had been bombed. Why not Hiroshima?

A Visit to Hiroshima

In the heart of Hiroshima—a modern city of just over a million people on Japan's Honshu island—lies a serene park with walking paths, green lawns, and leafy trees. It was created in 1949 as a way to remember the many lives lost in the world's first nuclear attack. At one end is the Hiroshima Peace Memorial (Genbaku Dome)—the only structure left standing on the site where the bomb was dropped. It is a skeleton now, but it was once the Hiroshima Prefectural Industrial Promotion Hall, a European-style building with the only domed roof in the city. A trading company was housed here, as well as a craft school. It was also a place for performances by tap dancers and comedians. For children, the land around the building was a playground, perfect for hide-and-seek and tag. Today, the ruins are as they were on August 6, 1945.

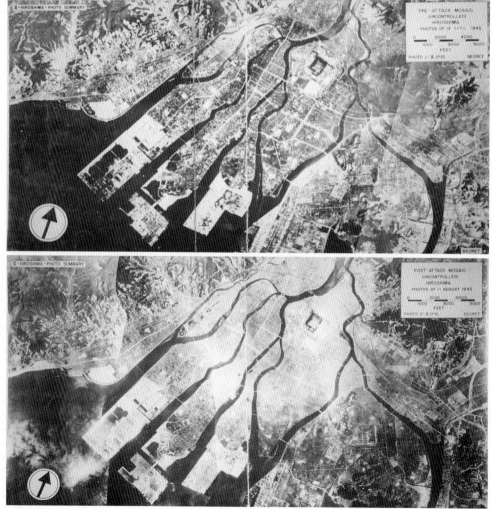

Top: Pre-attack view of Hiroshima on April 13, 1945   **Bottom:** Post-attack view of Hiroshima on August 11, 1945

Top left: *The remains of the Genbaku Dome (Atomic Bomb Dome) in Peace Memorial Park*
Top right: *A prewar photograph of Hiroshima's shopping district near the center of town*
Bottom: *Streetcars on Hiroshima streets on the morning of August 6, 1945*

The Hiroshima Peace Memorial Park lies over what was the neighborhood of Nakajima—an important part of Hiroshima and, hence, a natural target for the bomb. The busy streets around the Industrial Promotion Hall were once tightly lined with wooden shops and houses. You could buy kimonos, footwear, makeup, seaweed, eels, and oysters there. For lunch you might have a penny pancake bought on the street. You ate it fast because lunchtime was for marbles or menko cards. (One player puts a menko card on the ground, and the opponent tries to flip it by the way they throw down their card. Success meant keeping both cards.)

Hiroshima Castle was originally built in the 1590s but was largely destroyed by the bombing. It was rebuilt in 1958 and now houses a museum of Hiroshima's history before World War II.

There were two movie theaters in Nakajima, one that played American movies such as *King Kong*, and one that played Japanese movies, including lots of action films featuring samurai heroes. When there was no sound for the Japanese movies, storytellers would fill in, narrating the tale while the movie played.

If you were really lucky, your parents might take you to one of the local oyster boat restaurants. Or, better yet, to Nakajima's only Western-style restaurant, Café Brazil, where you could order coffee and rice omelets and curry.

And there was always the river. From spring to autumn, the doors of shops and houses were opened to catch the breezes coming off the water. In summer, you would find time for swimming or fishing for shrimp and eels. After the stores closed for the night, people would gather at the community bath, a large bathing pool. It was always busy, filled with patrons catching up on the news of the day until it closed at midnight.

Emperor Hirohito, 1901–1989

The Emperor

Shinto is a Japanese religion that incorporates the worship of ancestors, nature, and spirits. According to tradition, the position of emperor was created in the seventh century BCE, but it was probably later, during the fifth or sixth century. Emperors came to be known as Tenno, or "heavenly sovereign," based on the belief that they were descendants of Shinto Kami (spirits) and so were considered the sons of heaven. Today, emperors are viewed as human but are still very important in Japan. Although the emperor's political power is now limited, he is defined by the Constitution of Japan as being the symbol of the state and the unity of the country. (Although women were allowed to hold the role of emperor in the past, they are not currently permitted to do so.)

Left: *Tokugawa Ieyasu (1543–1616) was the founder and first shogun of the Tokugawa shogunate of Japan.* **Center:** *Emperor Meiji around the 1890s* **Right:** *Toyotomi Hideyoshi (1537–1598) was regarded as the second "Great Unifier" of Japan.*

Hiroshima had been founded as a castle town on the Ota River delta in 1589. Even before the war, life here and across Japan was changing. For hundreds of years, the country had been ruled by a shogun (a military general), feudal lords called *daimyos,* and samurai, members of a warrior class who gave the shogun power over the emperor. The last shogunate ended in 1868 with the Meiji Restoration, when the emperor Meiji was crowned. After that, Hiroshima grew fast. Soon it was the tenth-largest city in Japan and known for its progressive ways, especially in matters of education and teacher training. Japan was no longer a feudal society. It was becoming one of the most powerful nations in the modern world.

"After the Meiji Restoration, most of the country's provinces were replaced with prefectures, led by a governor who answered to the central government. When the first governor traveled to Hiroshima by boat around 1872, he and his family had to be carried to dry land. That left him determined to build a decent harbor for the city, but such a project cost a lot of money. My grandfather played an important role in raising the money for a harbor. Its construction eventually had an impact not anticipated at the time. In 1884, nobody was thinking of the harbor for military use—it was built for trade. But by the time of World War II, almost all personnel shipped to the battles in the Pacific left from Hiroshima. Our relatives would bring cold food and spread out a blanket in the park to see my cousins off to war. At first it was exciting, but my father had lived in California and knew the power of the United States. He was worried."
—Setsuko

The World Goes to War, 1939–1945

The Axis Powers

Between 1914 and 1918, the world was caught up in what people called the "war to end all wars." Tragically, they were wrong. That conflict is now called World War I because it was soon followed by the most destructive war in history, World War II.

Germany, which had been part of a group of countries that started the fighting in World War I, was defeated in 1918. It was left poor and demoralized. In 1933 the Nazi Party, led by Adolf Hitler, came to power. After experiencing years of devastating poverty, German citizens were eager for change. Hitler and the Nazi Party said that one way to improve living conditions was to return Germany to its former glory, to a time when "Aryans" (see sidebar) were the "superior race" and in control. If only there were no Jews, or Roma, or people who were homosexual, or people living with disabilities, Aryans could take their place as the world's leaders, he said.

In 1939 Germany invaded Poland. Great Britain and France responded by declaring war on Germany. World War II was fought between the Axis powers (Germany, Japan, and Italy, among others) and the Allied powers (Britain, France while unoccupied, the Soviet Union, the United States, and Canada among others).

map: World War II map and propaganda poster featuring the stereotypical Nazi "ideal": a blond Aryan German family of six, including a boy in a Hitler Youth uniform

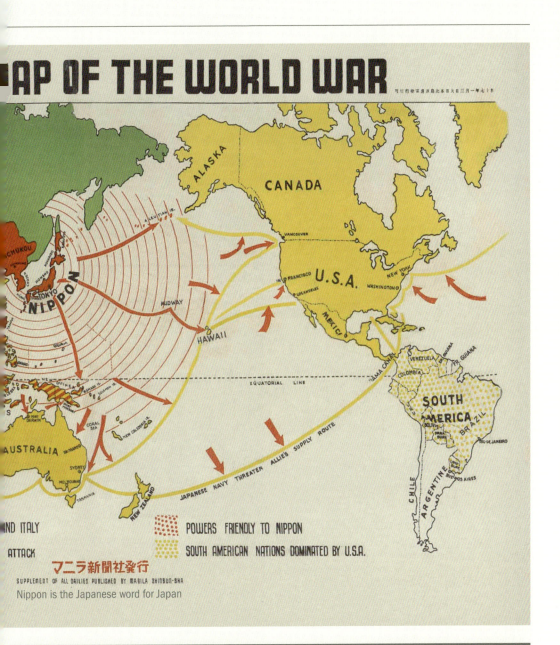

Who Is an Aryan?

Originally, the word *Aryan* referred to groups of people who spoke several related languages, including Indo-European ones. Now, however, the word has a different meaning. In the late nineteenth century, it began being used to refer to a mythical "race" of blue-eyed white people of northern European descent. The Nazi ideology falsely claimed superiority of the "Aryan race" over everyone else.

Japan in World War II

Japan is mountainous and has few of the resources, like oil, that military vehicles and battleships need. To gain more land and more resources, Japan became a colonizer, setting out to conquer other countries. Eventually, the Empire of Japan stretched throughout Southeast Asia and the Pacific for thousands of miles in all directions.

Japan invaded French Indochina (now known as Vietnam, Cambodia, and Laos) on September 22, 1940, and five days later joined Germany and Italy as an Axis power. With that, it entered World War II.

Why did Japan and Germany join together? After all, they are some 9,000 kilometers (5,600 miles) apart, and Nazis in Germany were racist. The few Japanese people who lived in Germany were poorly treated—for instance, they were forbidden to go to university. The answer may be that Japan and Germany admired one another's military strength or saw each other as global powers. Besides which, both countries wanted to defeat Britain, the Soviet Union, and the United States.

Japan was worried that the United States would try to stop Japan's takeover of countries in Southeast Asia, which would cut off its supply of war resources. Early in the war, it decided to attack the US Navy, hoping to sink enough ships to keep the United States from ever invading Japan.

Sunday, December 7, 1941 (December 8 in Japan, due to the time zone difference) was supposed to be a day of rest for the military at Naval Station Pearl Harbor in Hawaii. But at 7:55 a.m., Japanese fighter planes zoomed in without warning and attacked the US Pacific Fleet moored in the harbor. It is estimated that 2,403 Americans, including 68 civilians,

died. Nineteen US Navy ships, including eight battleships, were destroyed or badly damaged.

The next day, the United States declared war on Japan, thereby officially entering World War II. Over the next four years, the US Navy sank all of the Japanese aircraft, battleships, and cruisers that took part in the attack on Pearl Harbor.

Hardships of Daily Life

As the war went on, daily life in Japan grew harder. Clothes were rationed. Women were not allowed to wear skirts or high heels. Instead, they wore baggy pants—easier to move in during an emergency. People often slept in their clothes in case there was a bombing and they had to run to a shelter.

Food was rationed. Sugar was scarce. Rice was mixed with cracked wheat or whatever food was available. When people went out, they carried a first aid kit and a bag of roasted beans in case they were stranded during an attack.

Hiroshima's population shrank from around 380,000 to 245,000 as children were evacuated to temples and farms in the countryside north of the city.

Older schoolchildren were put to work to help with the war effort. They planted rice and potatoes on farms or were sent to factories to sew buttons onto soldiers' uniforms.

In the city, familiar streets became unrecognizable. People installed cement water tanks in front of their homes in case bombs designed to start fires were dropped. Some houses were pulled down to create

A Japanese military students' organization parades in front of Japanese officials and the German and Italian ambassadors in Tokyo in 1940.

Top: *Schoolgirls with rifles over their shoulders get insight into basic military training just before the outbreak of World War II.* **Left:** *Japanese children participate in simulated air raid emergencies in 1937.*

fire lanes—wide paths that, along with the rivers, would prevent the spread of fires if the city were bombed. Children in grades seven and eight—there were more than six thousand of them still in Hiroshima—worked near the center of the city to prepare the fire lanes.

Some boys became fighters. Fliers called Young Boy Pilots joined the air force training corps when they were just fourteen. By the time they were seventeen, eighteen, or nineteen, many had become *kamikazes*. The word *kamikaze* means "heavenly or divine wind." Kamikazes flew aircraft loaded with explosives and made suicidal crashes on enemy targets.

Everyone made sacrifices willingly, because it was an honor to work for the glory of the country.

"The Most Terrible Bomb"

A Silent Flash

The evening of Sunday, August 5, 1945, my older sister Ayako and her four-year-old son Eiji arrived in Hiroshima. They had come to town so Ayako could see a doctor about a problem with her eye. There was more food in the countryside, and she'd made and brought with her my mother's favorite dish of red bean paste in sticky rice. We had afternoon tea together in the sunny garden and enjoyed the rare treat. My father was annoyed that Ayako had come and wanted her to go back to the safety of her country home.

The usual air raid sirens blared throughout the night, but next morning the all clear was sounded. I got up at 6:30 a.m. to get ready for my first official day of work as a decoder.

The blue summer sky was cloudless. I walked to the railway station to meet my classmates. I was the leader of the group. We formed ranks. I gave the order—"Quick march"—and we paraded off to the army headquarters, a big wooden building about one and a half kilometers (one mile) from the center of Hiroshima.

At the door, we saluted the sentry. Major Yanai was in charge of the coding operations. We followed him to a large room on the second floor. He told us, "Girls, this is the way we dedicate our work to the emperor. Do your best!" Just as we replied, "Yes, we will do our best," the entire window filled with a blinding bluish-white flash.

Miles outside the city, people heard a thunderous roar, but I heard no explosion. There was just that silent flash. Together with the building, I was falling. I was knocked unconscious. When I came to, I found myself in darkness, buried under the debris of the collapsed building. I thought a bomb had dropped right on me.

I couldn't move. Though I knew I was facing death, all I felt was a strange calm. I heard the faint voices of the other girls whimpering, "Help me, Mother. I'm here. Help me, God."

Suddenly, someone's strong hand was shaking my shoulder. Then hands were loosening the timbers around me. I heard a man's voice. "Don't give up, keep pushing, keep moving." There was a glimmer of light to my left. The man said, "Don't give up. I'm trying to free you. You see the sunlight in the opening? Crawl toward it as quick as you can." I crawled out of the darkness. The building was on fire.

Only three of us girls survived. The other twenty-seven burned to death.

The Living and the Dead

My clothes were in bloody tatters. I had cuts and scratches all over me, but my arms and legs were still there. Horrified, I watched as streams of human beings shuffled away from the city. Parts of their bodies were missing. Their eyes had been liquified, their skin blackened, and strips of flesh hung like ribbons from their bones. There was an awful smell in the air: the stench of burnt human flesh. I have no words to describe it.

The strangest thing was the silence. You'd think that people would be panic-stricken, running, yelling. Instead, they moved in slow motion through the dust and smoke, gasping the words, "Water . . . give me water." Many simply dropped to the ground and died.

The three of us who'd managed to escape the building joined the ghostly procession. We walked to a hillside military training ground where we'd been told to go in case of emergency. It was about the size of two football fields. By the time we got there, the ground was covered with the injured, dying, and dead.

We looked around for doctors or nurses. There were none. Here, too, the injured whispered for water, "Help . . . please . . . give me water." We found a stream nearby. We had no buckets or containers, so we tore off our blouses, soaked them in the water, and ran back to the dying people. They sucked the moisture from the cloth, and even though they were in horrible pain, they thanked us.

A thousand students had been clearing fire lanes out in the open when the bomb exploded. Almost all of them died. One of the few survivors was my best friend, who was also called Setsuko. Most of her classmates had been blinded by the blast, but they could still hear. Our math teacher, Miss Yonehara, had them form a circle and sing. They sang the hymn "Nearer, My God, to Thee." She said, "If you can, try to stand and come near me. We will go to the nearby Red Cross hospital. Put your hands on my shoulder. I can support you." Setsuko obeyed, but as she touched her teacher's shoulder, the woman's skin came off. Setsuko could see the bone. Miss Yonehara lived for three or four days before she died.

The Days After

I am not sure how my parents were reunited, but I think they met up the next morning at a relative's house. In my memory, I can see my father and mother walking toward me. They'd heard that people from the military headquarters where I worked had escaped to the military training ground. I heard my name being called by a soldier: "Nakamura Setsuko!" I replied, "Here I am!" And there they were. All my father said was "Yokatta," which means "Thank goodness you're alive!" For a long time, we didn't say anything else.

We went to the relative's summer house. Ayako and Eiji were there. They had been crossing a bridge on their way to the doctor when the bomb fell. There was nothing to shield them. Somehow, they had been able to crawl back to our house, but there was no house there anymore. A neighbor saw them. She found a bottle of cooking oil to soothe their awful burns. The neighbor carried Eiji, who was nearly dead, while Ayako crawled along with the bottle of cooking oil in her arms to the summer house. By the time I saw them the next morning, their bodies were swollen to twice the normal size.

We stayed in that house for ten days while my sister and nephew lay dying. There was nothing we could do for them. We had no medicines. All we could do was try to ease their agony. Eiji would cry, "Grandma give Eiji boo-boo." Boo-boo is a child's word for water. I watched their blackened, swollen bodies being unceremoniously cremated in a ditch. I didn't cry. I couldn't. The memory of this has never left me.

Surrender

On August 15, soldiers went around the city shouting into megaphones that there would be an important announcement on the radio at noon. My father and I joined the crowds gathering on the hill. From loudspeakers in the tree branches came the emperor's voice. He said that he expected his subjects to bear the unbearable. Most people listened in silence. Nobody had ever heard the emperor's voice before. Though the loudspeakers crackled and the emperor used formal court language, we understood. Japan was surrendering. The war was over.

The day after the surrender, we moved to my uncle's house just outside the city. There was food for us, and some clothes, and a farmer's house where we could live. My uncle's wife and two daughters never returned from Hiroshima.

We spent most of our time looking for my sister-in-law, who had been in the center of the city supervising students at the time of the bombing. There were only ashes and broken tiles where our house once stood. Teacups and rice bowls had melted and were stuck together, but we were able to salvage an ornate clock in a cast-iron frame. Years later, I donated it to the Canadian War Museum in Ottawa. Though we searched for weeks, we never found my sister-in-law.

Numb

Much later, I learned that when something horrific happens to us, we sometimes go numb. The numbness serves a purpose. If I hadn't been numb, I couldn't have continued functioning in a world where I had lost my home, my family members, my friends, my school, and my city.

In mid-September, five weeks after the bombing, I was caught in a typhoon. I had to wade knee-deep through an area flooded with floating garbage and excrement. For the first time since the bombing, I broke down and sobbed. When I got home, drenched and exhausted, I cried out my misery to my father. He scolded me. "What right do you have to complain when we have life, each other, and a roof over our heads?" It was a life-changing moment; my father made me realize how fortunate I was to have survived.

His words forced me to come to terms with reality. People sometimes ask me why my experiences did not make me bitter. I think it was because the adult survivors around me showed such courage and goodness. I will never forget the many kindnesses I saw—injured people fetching water for the thirsty; the hungry sharing their meager portions of food; and those who'd lost almost everything ripping up scarce pieces of clothing for bandages.

My parents set a remarkable example. They never once complained. They'd lost everything yet were not defeated. Maybe that was their samurai heritage. I don't know. But that remark of my father's gave me the strength to resume life, to rebuild. That day marked the end of my emotional numbness. I faced the facts of our terrible misery. Now I was determined to carry on.

My school reopened in October in a hut up in the hills. When it rained, the noise of the drops on the corrugated tin roof was so loud we couldn't hear the teachers. With no glass in the windows, the wind blew in and we froze. But we didn't care; we were happy to be together again and to feel that life was getting back to normal.

That feeling of relief didn't last long. People who had survived the blast were beginning to come down with mysterious symptoms. We survivors didn't know then that we were facing the effects of radiation from the atomic bomb, including leukemia and other cancers. I experienced internal bleeding and diarrhoea. My gums bled. Like many others, I began to lose my hair. I didn't lose as much as some girls, who became completely bald. They'd appear at school wearing bonnets.

Then people quietly started dying—even those without any external sign of injury. They developed small purple spots on their bodies. Our teacher would say, "Miss So-and-So isn't with us today." Then we'd hear that she'd died. We knew that it was related to the purple spots. Every morning, we would check for them. If you had the spots, you were going to die.

Life Under Occupation

After the surrender, US and British Commonwealth forces, eventually numbering almost one million strong, occupied Japan. They set about changing the country with democratic ideas. Some of the changes were much needed, including the introduction of women's political and social rights and reforms in education. Traditional Japanese schools had emphasized obedience, memorization, and a standard, rigid curriculum, with little interaction between students and teachers. The United States introduced new textbooks. Classes became coed. Parents were allowed to vote for school boards.

Within days of the surrender, the occupying forces passed the Press Code. Writing about the atomic bomb as a scientific wonder was allowed, but anything that might be a criticism of the United States—like descriptions of the damage done to Hiroshima and Nagasaki—was forbidden. Anything—survivors' letters, diaries, films, photos, even medical records—that showed the horrible effects of the nuclear weapons was confiscated. Thousands of pieces of evidence were shipped to the United States. We were told that the American government and decision-makers did this so that there would be less anti-US feeling. But we Japanese thought it was because they didn't want the world to know the truth about what happens in a nuclear war.

A New Kind of Weapon

"We have discovered the most terrible bomb in the history of the world."
—U.S. president Harry S. Truman

American leaders believed that the only way they could get Japan to surrender would be to invade the country. However, they estimated that it would cost the lives of up to one million US soldiers and Allied prisoners of war. Instead of invading, President Truman decided to use a new weapon: the atomic bomb.

An atomic bomb's immense power is created by splitting an atom of the element uranium. Two hundred thousand Americans worked on what was called the Manhattan Project—a top-secret program dedicated to figuring out how the United States could use atomic energy to make a devastating bomb before Germany or any other enemy did.

The first test bomb was exploded in the New Mexico desert on July 16, 1945. The temperature at the heart of the explosion was three times hotter than the center of the sun. The test went well, but many of the scientists involved were troubled. They could tell how much damage the bomb could do.

By the time the Americans finished the bomb, Germany had already surrendered, and the war in Europe was over. Japan was defeated too, but the emperor had still not surrendered. The United States decided to bomb Hiroshima and, three days later, the city of Nagasaki. Was it necessary in order to end the war or was it an experiment to see what the atomic bomb could do?

The devastation and destruction after the dropping of the atomic bomb on Hiroshima.

Little Boy and Fat Man

The bomb that the United States dropped on Hiroshima on August 6, 1945, had been given a nickname: Little Boy. Little Boy had a parachute attached to slow its fall so that the Enola Gay, the plane piloted by Colonel Paul Tibbets, could get away before the bomb exploded.

The blast was equivalent to 14,500 metric tonnes (16,000 tons) of TNT exploding. It sent a pulse of thermal energy rippling across the city that flattened 13 square kilometers (5 square miles). Ground temperatures reached 4,000 degrees Celsius (7,200 degrees Fahrenheit).

On August 9, the United States dropped a second atomic bomb, this time on Nagasaki. The Americans called this one Fat Man. It killed 60,000 to 80,000 people, about half when the bomb dropped and the others from radiation in the days and months that followed.

Left: A high-angle view of the explosion of the atomic bomb on Hiroshima **Top right:** S. Dike examines the fitness of the unit containing the atomic bomb, Little Boy, in August 1945. **Bottom right:** The type of nuclear weapon detonated over Hiroshima was about 71 cm (28 in.) in diameter and 304 cm (120 in.) long and weighed about 4,082 kg (9,000 lb.).

A survivor of the Hiroshima nuclear bomb sits in the midst of the destroyed buildings.

After Little Boy exploded, Hiroshima was in flames. Large clouds of dust and ash rose, turning the day darker and darker. That morning there had been no wind. Now brisk winds blew every which way. New fires sprang up, and they spread fast.

Black smoke and dust blocked out the sun. Clumps of smoke started pushing up through the dust. In the northwestern part of the city, marble-sized drops of black sticky rain began to fall. The raindrops were condensed moisture from the tower of dust, heat, and fission fragments that had risen miles into the sky. The injured and parched people drank the black rain pouring onto them. The rain was radioactive—which means it produced a harmful energy that causes severe damage to humans (such as burns and cancers) and to the environment.

Early in the evening, a naval launch moved slowly up and down the city's seven rivers. It stopped here and there: at the sandpits where hundreds of wounded people lay, trying to cool their burnt bodies in the water; at the crowded bridges; and at a park to which many people had fled. Somebody shouted through a megaphone: "Be patient! A naval hospital ship is coming to take care of you." No such ship arrived.

A whirlwind ripped through the wasteland of Hiroshima. Huge trees crashed; small ones, uprooted, flew through the air. The whirlwind eventually moved over the rivers, where it sucked up the water into a waterspout and eventually spent itself.

Everything was still smoldering when the next day dawned. The houses on the outskirts of town were damaged, with shattered windows and collapsed walls. But the heart of the city, three square kilometers (one square mile) of the city was a brown-red scar. The ghostly frames of twisted bicycles and the shells of streetcars and automobiles were all that remained of bustling traffic. The rivers didn't flow. They were choked with bodies.

At one hospital, where there were six hundred beds, ten thousand wounded and dying people begged the doctors, themselves injured, for help. Others were nowhere near even that scrap of help. They died in fires, or from radiation, or were buried in rubble.

The five thousand children who had been evacuated before the bomb fell didn't know that the city had been wiped out. They came back to a scene of devastation, alone and confused without parents or shelter.

They ran wild, doing whatever they could to survive. Many of them crowded around the train station. Sometimes they resorted to criminal activity like pickpocketing. There was no government support for them. With extraordinary goodwill, survivors volunteered to help. Some opened their homes to take in orphans. Other survivors opened orphanages.

It was a lonely, hard life for children, waiting for their parents—most of whom would never return. Eventually, many of the children lost hope. Some never spoke of the war again.

A toddler sits crying amidst the rubble left by the atomic explosion in Hiroshima on August 6, 1945.

Japanese children look at the Genbaku Dome in Hiroshima Peace Memorial Park on the eve of the 55th anniversary of the atomic bomb blast in the city. Some 140,000 people were killed in the world's first atomic bombing.

"The Silence Lifts"

The *Hibakusha*

When the Occupation ended in 1952, people gradually shed their emotional numbness. Before that, survivors had felt abandoned by the Japanese government, which had not provided any medical or financial help. We were *Hibakusha*—explosion-affected persons.

Hibakusha pressured the government for help. They wrote memoirs and articles. They drew and painted what they remembered. They began making public speeches and involving themselves in political action. By doing so, they not only helped themselves recover psychologically but also began to warn the world about the danger of nuclear weapons.

The Atomic Age Is Born

The destruction of Hiroshima and Nagasaki did not warn people away from the use of nuclear power. In fact, in the United States and elsewhere, people were excited about the "peacetime" possibilities: the bomb could blow away mountains for mining, alter the course of rivers, wipe out the Great Barrier Reef to make shipping easier. Comic books with titles like Atomic War! and Atom-Age Combat began to appear.

On March 1, 1954, America detonated a nuclear weapon with an explosive yield of 15 megatons over the Bikini Atoll in the Marshall Islands. The purpose was to test the potential effectiveness of the weapons on naval warships. The blast was seen in Okinawa, 4,200 kilometers (2,600 miles) away. The fallout covered 18,100 square kilometers (7,000 square miles).

On the fishing boat Lucky Dragon No. 5, twenty-three Japanese crewmen, and their cargo of tuna, were exposed to radiation by the American test. The bomb test over the Bikini Atoll enraged Japan. Millions of people in Japan signed a petition to ban the atomic bomb.

Left: An aerial view of a mushroom cloud from an atomic bomb detonated in Bikini Atoll in the Pacific
Right: People of Bikini Atoll carry their belongings in the evacuation of the island before the atomic bomb test in 1946. Twenty-three nuclear devices were detonated in the Bikini vicinity between 1946 and 1958 at seven test sites.

THE ILLUSTRATED LONDON NEWS

SATURDAY, JUNE 29, 1946.

TARGET FOR ANNIHILATION: AN ATOM-BOMBER'S VIEW OF BIKINI ATOLL, IN THE PACIFIC OCEAN, WITH THE FLEET OF WARSHIP VICTIMS ASSEMBLED IN THE LAGOON.

On Monday next, July 1, the most powerful atom bomb yet developed—a duplicate of the bomb which pulverised Nagasaki on August 9, 1945—is timed to be dropped on a fleet of "guinea-pig" warships anchored in the lagoon of Bikini Atoll, in the Pacific Ocean. The bomb is to be dropped by a Super-Fortress from a height of 30,000 ft., aimed at the "bull's-eye" battleship *Nevada*, which has been painted a bright orange-red. The experiment, primarily designed to determine the future of sea power under the threat of atom-bombing, will be watched by official observers from ships, aircraft and neighbouring islands. Its effects will be awaited with anxiety by a world whose security has already been severely shaken by the advent of atomic power. (This important experiment is further illustrated on subsequent pages.)

A New Focus

After I graduated from college in Japan, I received a scholarship to study in Virginia. I arrived about five months after the United States hydrogen bomb tests at Bikini Atoll. I was interviewed by newspaper reporters about Hiroshima and my feelings about the hydrogen bomb, a thousand times more destructive than the atomic bomb.

I said that Hiroshima and Nagasaki should have marked the end of nuclear experiments, not the beginning. As soon as my remarks were published, the hate mail began. I got letters telling me: "Go home!" and "Remember Pearl Harbor!" I received death threats. At times I could not go to class, so I moved into a professor's house. But I vowed I would not be silenced. My life as an activist had begun.

I had met Canadian Jim Thurlow in Japan, and we had fallen in love. His parents gave us their blessing to get married, but it took my parents a year to accept the fact that I was not marrying a Japanese man. Our wedding took some planning. My first choice was to get married in Canada, but there was a law against Asian immigration into Canada except for close relatives of Canadian citizens. In Virginia, there was a law against interracial marriage; that is, marriage between races. So we got married in Washington, DC, and moved to Toronto. I enrolled at the University of Toronto and received a master's degree in social work.

Many Canadians, and particularly the press, saw my experience in Hiroshima as a good human interest story but nothing more. They were unwilling to acknowledge that nuclear weapons were a global problem. It was easy to look at atomic bombs as a Japanese or an American concern, forgetting that the American government used Canadian uranium to make the bomb or that Canada's prime minister, Mackenzie King, had remarked that he was glad the bomb had been dropped on the Japanese and not on the white races of Europe.

Whenever I was asked to give a speech or an interview, I did what I could to inform Canadians. But it wasn't until I took part in a disarmament conference in Hiroshima in 1974 that I became actively involved. There, in the city I grew up in, I met other survivors, brave people who had transcended their personal tragedies and were devoting themselves to peace. While peace and disarmament had been important to me before, I realized that they'd now be the focus of my life.

My Fight for Peace

Jim and I had a happy marriage for over fifty-five years. We had two fine, healthy sons, Peter and Andrew. I had a successful career as a social worker with the Toronto District School Board.

Nevertheless, the longer I live, the angrier I get about the bombing of Hiroshima and Nagasaki. Such needless suffering! And no leader has expressed an apology. I am not angry at American people, but I believe that American leaders committed crimes against humanity. They knew what would happen and wanted to experiment. During the seven years of occupation after the end of the war, they lied about the need to drop the atomic bomb. As for the Japanese government, it had been at war for years before World War II, colonizing countries like Korea and Taiwan. That made me angry too.

I was determined that the world had to know about the horrors of an atomic bomb so that such a calamity would never occur again. In Toronto, I gathered a group of trusted friends from various walks of life, including clergy, scientists, lawyers, a sociologist, and a writer as well as another survivor from Hiroshima. Together we developed a program of public consciousness-raising, including an exhibition of photographs, loaned to us by the City of Hiroshima, to commemorate the thirtieth anniversary of the bombing. Since that event in 1975, I've also spoken extensively in the United States, Japan, Britain, and other European countries. I've addressed the United Nations many times.

I became involved with the International Campaign to Abolish Nuclear Weapons (ICAN) in Canada. ICAN is made up of more than six hundred groups, mostly community-level grassroots, in one hundred countries. On behalf of ICAN, I have testified before world leaders, and after much work by many dedicated people, on July 7, 2017, the United Nations voted on the adoption of the Treaty on the Prohibition of Nuclear Weapons (TPNW)—a promise by those who sign to not develop, test, produce, acquire, possess, stockpile, or use the threat of nuclear weapons. Nuclear weapons have always been immoral. Now they are illegal. In 2017, our work was recognized with the Nobel Peace Prize and I had the honor of giving the Nobel lecture upon receiving the prize.

"Tea cups and rice bowls were melted together, but we were able to salvage an ornate clock in a cast-iron frame. I have it still"

In my acceptance speech when ICAN was awarded the Nobel Peace Prize, I repeated the words I heard while trapped in the smoldering rubble: I kept pushing, I kept moving toward the light. I invite you to do the same.

   In the Peace Memorial Park in Hiroshima, the cenotaph inscription reads "Rest in peace; evil will not be repeated." This has become the vow of the survivors—to end the threat of nuclear weapons so that what happened in Hiroshima and Nagasaki never happens again. Only when this is accomplished will we know that the grotesque deaths of our loved ones have not been in vain. Only then will our own survival have meaning.

Ban the Bomb!

Top: In one of the first marches for the international "ban the bomb" movement, 5,000 people from Sweden, France, the United States, Japan, and many other countries demonstrated in 1960.
Bottom: Hiroshima survivors Miyako Matsubara and Hirosama Hanabusa join the Aldermaston March in London is 1962.

In 1958, the Campaign for Nuclear Disarmament (CND) formed in England to oppose the use of nuclear weapons and other weapons of mass destruction. A global peace movement soon erupted. Over the next thirty years, people around the world protested the production of nuclear weapons and nuclear power. The aim: to find other kinds of energy; to warn people about environmental hazards; to make sure that nuclear industry workers were safe; and, above all, to ban the use of nuclear weapons in war.

On June 12, 1982, an estimated one million protesters converged on New York City's Central Park to demand an end to nuclear weapons. In October 1983, an estimated three million people across Western Europe came together to protest against nuclear weapons. And in Britain, four hundred thousand people participated in what may have been, at that time, the largest demonstration in the country's history.

Is it possible to ban the bomb? After all, isn't war all about violence and wiping out the enemy? In fact, many weapons have been banned because of the awful damage they can do to all living things and to the earth itself. Countries that break the laws against certain kinds of weapons can be tried in national courts or by the International Criminal Court in The Hague, The Netherlands.

A Call to Action

At the time of writing, 167 countries have either signed the Treaty on the Prohibition of Nuclear Weapons or agreed to its terms. None of the countries that already have nuclear weapons voted at all.

Nine of the countries that did not sign the treaty have about 12,500 nuclear warheads among them. These include, in order from most to least weapons, Russia, the United States, China, France, the United Kingdom, Pakistan, India, Israel, and North Korea. Each of these weapons can cause enormous destruction; many are much larger than Little Boy or Fat Man. These are the chilling facts: Nuclear weapons are designed for mass murder of civilians. They do terrible, permanent harm to the environment. They are a waste of financial resources—in 2022, the nuclear nations wasted $82.9 billion on nuclear weapons.

There is still work to be done.

Logo for Peace
The nuclear disarmament movement had a logo that has come to mean peace. It was designed by Gerald Holtom in 1958 and is based on the semaphore symbols "N" for nuclear and "D" for disarmament. (Semaphore is a system of sending messages by holding two flags, poles, or even your arms in certain positions that represent an alphabetic code.)

What Can You Do?

1. Have hope! We have succeeded in banning other weapons, including mines, mustard gas, cluster bombs, and chemicals. There is no reason why we can't stop nuclear weapons.

2. Learn as much as you can about nuclear arms and the threat they pose. You don't need to be an expert, but information is power and having power helps.

3. Speak up against the bomb in letters to newspapers and politicians, and on social media.

4. Join others who are making a difference. Together we can end the threat.

Appendix:
Japan at War Timeline

1894–1895 Japan becomes an imperial power when it defeats China in the First Sino-Japanese War. Korea is colonized by Japan, and China gives up Taiwan to Japan. Japanese military power makes Japan ready to dominate the region.

1904 Japan is victorious in a war against Russia.

1910 Korea is annexed by Japan. (Annexation is when one state forcibly acquires and claims legal title over another state's territory. Territorial control is declared by the occupying power. The other side has no say.)

1914–1918 Japan joins the Allies, which included Great Britain, Russia, France, and eventually the United States, against Germany in World War I.

1924 The United States passes the Immigration Act, barring certain Asian immigration to the United States.

1929 A worldwide economic depression, lasting until about 1939, arouses nationalist feelings in Japan and elsewhere, stressing traditional values and ways of life.

1931 Japan invades and occupies Manchuria in northeast China, renaming it Manchukuo.

1933 Japan withdraws from the League of Nations—an international organization with a mission of maintaining peace—after being condemned for occupying Manchukuo.

1937–1945 Japan invades mainland China. The Second Sino-Japanese War sees violent battles in Shanghai, Beijing, and the capital city Nanjing.

1939–1945 War breaks out in Europe in what would come to be known as World War II. With the fall of France to Nazi Germany in 1940, Japan moves to occupy French Indochina.

1941 Japan attacks the US Pacific Fleet at Pearl Harbor, Hawaii. The next day, the United States and its allies declare war on Japan.

1941–1942 Japan occupies the Philippines, Dutch East Indies, Burma, and Malaya. The United States defeats the Japanese at the Battle of Midway and starts "island-hopping" to cut the Japanese supply lines from these countries.

1944 US forces come close enough to Japan to start bombing large cities.

1945 The atomic bomb is dropped on Hiroshima and Nagasaki. Emperor Hirohito surrenders and gives up his divine status. Japan is placed under US and British Commonwealth forces occupation.

1947 Japan renounces war, pledging not to maintain armed forces. The emperor is given ceremonial status.

1951 Japan signs a peace treaty with the United States and forty-seven other nations.

1952 The US military occupation of Japan ends when the treaty comes into effect.

A group of Tachikawa Ki-36 reconnaissance aircraft of the Imperial Japanese Army fly near Mount Fuji in the early 1940s.

Sources

Books
Burgan, Michael. *Hiroshima and Nagasaki.* Mankato, Minnesota: Capstone Press, 2019

Green, Joan M., Natalie Little, and Brenda Protherone. *Your Voice and Mine 2: A Silent Flash.* Toronto: Holt Rinehart, Winston, 1987.

Hersey, John. *Hiroshima.* New York: A.A. Knopf, 1946. [The entire contents of the book originally appeared in *The New Yorker.*]

Law, Ricky. *Transnational Nazism, Ideology, and Culture in German-Japanese Relations*, 1919–1936. Cambridge, England, 2019.

Ross, Stewart. *Hiroshima.* Britannica Digital Learning, 2012.

Movies
Director and Writer: Masaaki Tanabe. *Message from Hiroshima*, 2015.

Director: Susan Strickler. *The Vow from Hiroshima*, Bullfrog Films, 2019.

Interviews
Interviews with Setsuko Thurlow in Toronto, 2023 through 2024

Image Credits

11 Illus. in: Views & costumes of Japan by Stillfried & Andersen. Yokohama: Stillfried & Andersen [ca. 1877, p. 5]. Retrieved from Library of Congress; **16** U.S. Strategic Bombing Survey. Pacific Survey. Physical Damage Division. (09/1945 - 04/1946); **17 tl** All Canada Photos /ICP, inacamerastock / Superstock; **17 tr** War Department. U.S. Strategic Bombing Survey. Pacific Survey. Physical Damage Division. (09/1945 - 04/1946); **17 b** Photographer: Shigemi Hamamoto; **18 t** DXR/Wikimedia, CC BY-SA 4.0; **18 b** Universal History Archive/ UIG / Bridgeman Images; **19** from left Portrait of Tokugawa Ieyasu (1543-1616), Japanese school, 17th century; All Canada Photos/JTVintage/Glasshouse Images; Osaka City Museum of Fine Arts; **20–21** Manila Shinbun-sha. Original from The Beinecke Rare Book & Manuscript Library. Digitally enhanced by rawpixel; **21** inset Shawshots / Superstock; **22–23** The National WWII Museum; **24** Underwood Archives/UIG / Bridgeman Images; **25 t** SZ Photo / Scherl / Bridgeman Images; **25 b** Underwood Archives/UIG / Bridgeman Images; **42–43** All Canada Photos/Image Asset Management/Superstock; **44 l** 4X5 Collection / Superstock; **44 tr** National Museum of the U.S. Navy; **44 br** Los Alamos Scientific Laboratory, Harry S. Truman Library & Museum; **45** Harry S. Truman Library & Museum; **46** Pictures from History / Bridgeman Images; **47** REUTERS/Susumu Toshiyuki / Bridgeman Images; **56** Photo by Jim Allen; **58 l** Curtis Le May Papers / Library of Congress; **58 r** All Canada Photos/Everett Collection; **59** All Canada Photos/ Illustrated London News Ltd/Mary Evans Picture Library; **60 t** All Canada Photos/Everett Collection/Superstock; **60 b** KEYSTONE Pictures USA, Keystone Press / Superstock; **63** KEYSTONE Pictures USA, Keystone Press / Superstock.